First published 2019
by Subbed In
www.subbed.in

© Jason Gray 2019

Book design by Michael Sun
Cover design by Dan Hogan
Original template by Sam Wieck
Text set in 8pt Domaine Text

First edition

Printed and bound in Birraranga (Melbourne)

National Library of Australia Cataloguing-in-Publication:
Gray, Jason
HAUNT (THE KOOLIE) / Jason Gray.
ISBN: 978-0-6481475-9-6 (paperback)

Subbed In 010

All rights reserved.

This book is copyright. Apart from any fair dealing for the purposes of research, criticism, study, review or otherwise permitted under the Copyright Act, no part of this book may be reproduced by any process without permission. Inquiries should be addressed to Subbed In: hello@subbed.in

I acknowledge and pay respect to the traditional custodians of the land on which this poetry (a work of fiction) was written—land that was never ceded and was stolen from the Dharug and Gadigal-Wangal people. I give thanks and appreciation to Dharug and Eora, and wish to thank First Nations artists, friends and family, for their humility and leadership.

— Jason Gray

MALCONTENTS PAGE (FOR PLAYAS ONLY)

Choose Your Psycho-Realm:

--> *Narcissphere*
Psychopath Zone
Sociopath Skies

Choose Your Character (The Other Will Be Your Shadow):

Playa Zero
Disembodied Spirit absorbed by Your Psycho-Realm

--> *Playa One*
Florent – Wannabe Searcher, Misfit, not Hero, not Anti-Hero

HAUNT (THE KOOLIE)

Jason Gray

Welcome to the Narcissphere

Koolie kids are the scapegoats
All too clever
and liberated. Appreciators are
The scapegoats

Small, loved details are petty
Unless they are aimed and shot.
Received like a bullet, bogan-bigot
No Gun November might help.

Welcome back, eternal return
Welcome home to grief-sick (5G)
Welcome to the Narcissphere.
It's always your fault, adult, in a slavescape.

->->-> WHITEWASH

Granny Flat, Boom

I guess I live here now
Sapien cottage
boomer land, evergreen landlord, over-cooked-ruler Orc.
An individual unit,
but a solid groupie
Every neoliberal second
I'm like tik tik boomin'
counting Koolie time
Errr, like the playground Sirrr,
just go
BOOM.
A wise one, I guess, maybe sometimes
educated misfit, busted by
hip pokit squeeze, the only way.
Manifesting housing dreams, like Mumm-Ra
on the BoysTown lottery, glossy fold-outs
snorting the suburban mainline
bored, off work on non-weekends.
Festy sneakster tricks, pleasing the god of high anarchy
Welcome to the Goodshow
Blame the Koolie kids, the nanny-state.
This is the Sugar Daddy state
Creepy Gaze Haze!
Vampire Goons Only.

Black Dog, Brown Pup

A scruffy hoodie Curly Top lad
mown down but not sewn up
Unscrawny, a hoon?
Not even,
often stitched up.
Forced dreams,
broken into @ never-dawn.
Bloody productive, packaged
like a scoffing CEO, down
human resources, down
mouthfuls
Pale Cannibal Overdose
Double-Think garage,
Baulko Balcony! I am
fluffy mongrel, hipster mutt
playing @ Koolie daydreaming,
procrastinating by
picking up after every dream-houser,
holiday-rouser in multiple moneyed shires
of Old Sydney Town,
Flux City blushing
snob-side
for the wrong reasons.
Parading thieves like CEOS,
not friends. *Je suis chaud*
IDENTITY FRAUD!

Day One, the Landlord-Boss' Smile

Hello my Koolie
Hello my child
Bless bless
this phantom
pantomime
address.
And we are like family
Clean, clean
Fresh, fresh
I want my house
Less drudge / hot mess.
This is My Land
My children return seldom, eternal
My parents are gone, eternal
I am the great survivor
You are my child
I will address you thusly
Forever my child
Great-great grateful!
Be a good boy, Florent
And I will show you
the secrets
O' my owning!
An invisible smarm-glow
And no position description
delivered
under the door light,
casual caress

of slipper-scraped concrete
A Secret Film Treatment:
Little cottage in the wood
Little man @ the window stood... #
Welcome to the Laughing Hills
A shipwrecked pirate
White man
on land he claims to own
No identity other than battle
Passed down, passed on
Eternal nostalgia for nothingness
Lies adorn,
vicious ghost ships abound
when we join them on deck
the mythic ships (dis)appear.
canned laughter, applause
Come little rabbit, come with me
Happy we shall be. #
Raise your hands to the sky
And Fill Yourself
With the Power
of Cumulus Cloud Nonsense!
soft laughter, coughing

Cooked, Cleaned

I cook and clean
for the main-house royals
The landlord-boss, Mr Oz,
gives precariat chex,
bearing deathly bronze chest,
as I unmess I,
competent sheen, dying spleen
lame and obvious as can be
recycle Choice, Woman's Day
and sexist sports magazines.
Accept not-city, not here
I sleep in sweats
and grind fish teeth and
Wish for a Brown Town,
Wish for a Brown City
Can it be Parra, time to ourselves,
And actually see each other?
Unzom unity
A purity, bit dusty
And rusty, forking mortgage zombies
Endless holidays in their tent and Kombi.
But I don't want to judge
Don't want to embitter
I am happy to live here
As a waged housesitter.
I will live this lie,
hope not a dying day
As I watch HBO
home alone –
no buddy-crim duo stars
hand hidden, Target trackies –

Serotonin Search!:
Is This A Cure For Depression?
Foraging away.
I am mundane and I hate myself for it
As much as I allow myself to hate
Being that like any emotional energy
especially Nehh-Gah-Tiv,
more frowned upon
like a teacher's temples.
Emotion rarely rakes in fat cash-flow
unless you go viral.
I broke up with
the Fear of Not Being Cool Enough
and Fear of Not Being My Parents' Dream Child
let alone accepting the partial flux
of ever-changing
cycle of perception
of most relationships.
Vulnerability is a privilege
Sometimes it doesn't make
immigrant parents happy
But treating family, any immigrant-parents
Like pure constituency
Would, like, sicken
me stress-thickened blood.
To be cool enough
Accepted enough
To be boring, to make just enough
To have time
And not consider everything
a gross, middling production
is not a luxury
I can have
while living off
the necessity
of cooking and cleaning.

Infection / Koolie-Aid

Back in the day
Teenage years rolled on and bullshit matured
I became adept @ returning to the original sources
Infection and deprivation, permeating
brain and threatened to strike you
aggression, rage fists
In a world of haves and have-nots, I wish 4 sanity,
or at least a nice reservoir of zombie peace
in a bigotry-eaten country
seeded by
world @ war
All generations are war generations
BOOM
If the Cool-Kid Sapiens lose it.
No matter what acid rain
market falls seep from above
into fake-news drafts and Facebook profiles,
or economic trickster-corralling – Baby Boomer, Generation X, Y, Z –
designed by Demon Inc.
to divide and shred
history and heads,
We Koolies All, Plebs
Infection Kin.

Mr Gopal: Run Out Fiasco!

Back in the Day, in my town
Mr Gopal was run out.
Fiasco! Too Brown, Too Asian
My Mum, on the scene, reports.
Gaz O'Leary smashed
my lunchbox. I dobbed,
he mooned me. His bum
not wiped properly. Miss Dove,
our Year One teacher scolded
smiles politely / whispers instructions
Held his wrist
all the way to the toilet,
not just the naughty corridor,
blue bags and rain hoodies,
class on script: *laugh like kooka-toos
on red cordial* Miss Dove glared bindies @ you.
Ya Flashed Dobber!
on her way to investigate
the possibility of Gaz
in public underwear.
Back in the Day, in my town
Mr Gopal was run out.
Fiasco! Too Brown, Too Asian.
My Mum, on the scene, reports
The Mabelas, Jo'burg fam, Bella Vista settlers
received no cute wordplay. Ignored!
in queues to hand over money,
@ Castle Towers, @ Black Stump.

Did not ask for Lord's Prayer stricken
from daily assembly routine.
Niceling Freshie Blame Flames!
The Otherrr, smoky mist.
Back In the Day, In My Town –
Mr Gopal Was Run Out of Town.
White bogans: Too Brown / Too Asian,
My Mum, on the scene, reports
Weaponised offence, illegal:
Giveaway Stuff,
Curb-Kicker!
You don't want, they don't want
Vote no on handouts.

He who asks bowls last
Some folks claim love, claim how-used-to-be:
Nostalgia Egalitaria!
Some folks, tough-nut-parrots, kids
not-bullies, blackbird brinkin'
Advance Assault Fair
But Fuck the Police?
Brother, amirite
Negative Gearing Lite.
Some folks, tough-nut-parrot-kids
not-bullies, blackbird brinkin'
But Fuck the Police?
Some folks claim love, claim how-used-to-be:
Love.
I'm just a Koolie on nana naps
cleaning main house
more than granny flat.
Bro, rant over. Dig
Skull Island scary
Unknown, misty
land-chunk forebodey!

Greyscale Hillz

Castle Peaks pubbers!
Chatty-mouth chimney-sweeps of the Other Shire,
adult children who fear dark screens, dangerous
animals, ghosts stalking Coloured banter
Cohabitate my Granny Flat, just a sec.
Accompany me down the hill,
Wrong-side-of-the-tracks

under surveillance cams
where conversation replays dodgy.
Bashed Man Bleeds: Fears Supermarket Lights,
Aging in Vain, Hobbles Home.
Checkout kids swipe bin lids, buckets
for the wise, unsik mansion-dwellers
on pallid hillcrest
where joggers dream humble –
kicking off their shoes, kickin' it, weekend party bowls
under orange noir lamps,
how many clams, how many shams?
You see Black Panther? – twice, mate.
Always mention Kung-Fu Kenny,
Never discover Mauritius.
Not Mad-A-Gaslight-Scar!
Not Meet-Jah-May-Ka!
We Koolies All, fragments
slammin' the meat tray
winnings, charcoal residue
grill scraped steak juice,
licked blood-bubble. "Maaate!"
RSL Champ says to me, or does he
Is it not for me?
Asks to buy my skin-colour
If I am Waleed Aly or I know him.
As if, Dead God at his worst
dropped down a few planes, bombs,
Curb-Kicker, sidekick to our brains.
Beatnik Grog-Cheeked Bloke warbles
@-me, blow-in nightmare of New South Queensland
Colony,
greasy silver-spoon spatulas.
Suburban mainstream yachts grow, giant
weeds in driveways, outlaw
gutter trophies, never seem to

Like! Find water?
But: I am Black enough to hold
the Whiteness in me
on me and @-me, account without counting
a graceless film-fade into seething light
hide colour, enlighten or die
settling, whiny-rewind VHS scores
(At Aussie, we'll save you!)
Brown Oz my skin
and all around me, brown wizardry
my darting irises swirl
a hazel hum tinged green –
find water via old soul, old body, old movies.
But again, gentle reminders:
I am not a dripping watercolour-gum mini-series,
not '90s tree-change drama,
left to char on squashed ciggie-bushfire,
not a quarry of deadwood song,
not a clearing
for Whitewashed doof.
Not a Neighbourhood Watch

cautionary tale boof
Not a fake-celeb for couch-bashers
to burp firelighters and twigs
@ tea, I'm a Koolie, I like you
too much caffeine, hard work
(brown Oz my skin)
Recognise certain kinds,
Unsik-Wasted Only.

Approximation of Hip-Hop and Grunge Phenomena

O, the trade-offs I barely witness
Callous joy / man-made flames
Shattering asphyxiation, non-masthead
Rope shards burning, burnt-sugar portal cells
saccharine black-ish, girl-ish soul.
Other Dimensional brain spell,
kerbside clean-up city,
roller door, my childhood drawbridge.
Dust and mites and mould,
itching to sabotage eyeballs
Undissected Class dismissed, unresurrected.
HSC Club: *he was, on-ly, sev'teen.*
Survive. Adult, have not
and fall, Sydney fireball
I am your multicultural remains

I am better off West
Leaf-shadowed footpaths, starry nights are truest here
My blighted curse lifted in the mystery
of shopping cart, unmown grass
A missing hermit, homeless myth like me –
scavenging, fake avenging Koolie –
averages out to a tundra
unhallowed, unfollowed, marked X, tatty clothes
A childless map, grunting
Crunched taut by travel
Flipped to grovel,
face-down grommet, booked
and guttered, unravelled second-hand pot smoke
memory-stacker/unslacker. First-hand everyman
Nobody sticks overtime
or underemployment on me
brain broken into by
cherry-pickin'

'Burban Beef-Cheek Beasts Matter.
Plundered and pillaged
parking lottery, mettle summons
kindly spirits, soothe hot capillaries
Camo-country-flage-mile to unseed Ulysses
brush off scratchy sand flecks from grey tiles
chicken curry and faratha to nourish
The dregs of the anniversary,
Honeyed yoghurt.

A Cricketer is Dead

A cricketer is dead. He was young and male and White.
Hysterical Realism! Australia will notice now.
I was never a Koolie kid but I was forced to drop Damon
    Hedgeley from the 14A's.
The Coach, a History teacher, told the Captain, who told me.
Down the chain.
I also had to tell him his replacement and he stormed off
down the Stockland Drive hill just like he stormed off
years later from that Gosford pub
    after Grousetime lost the battle of the bands
and his hipster friends whinged about him leaving,
behind his hilariously V-shaped back, which also left.
Jokes, it was a fine spine. I can be random-superficial too for
jokes
I was in the A's cricket team but wasn't
    what they were used to so didn't bother with them
enough to be worthy of more than non-racism – Friends,
Frieeends,
actual friends, recruited
    from the Frankenstein Monster Musical team.
But I can deffo drive cricketers home – it was clear

*I was allowed to be near and beneath
the fascist, failed sports-star musicians, the pretty White girls.
I'd do as I was told, unlike Damon?
I opened the batting for three years after Damon was dropped,
even though I said I was a bowler all-rounder, and faced
bowlers who bowled as fast as Aussie cricketers,*

    rep kids power-brats who only played club cricket for
""""shits and giggles""""" —

    *another inexplicable White ritual
that is better not to ask about
You might have to bowl last, like OMG!,
or get brown-eyed or atomic wedgied
Or get forced to brown-eye like Gaz or atomic-wedgie yourself.*
Like om, there is no g.
Omm, nom, nom.
Nominal actions nominate defeat
jokes
Can a ball get through the gap in this helmet, but?
Nah, you'll be right, Champ
Sometimes, it is better to ignore White people,
even if you are one. It is invisibility
they crave. *A Cricketer is Dead. A true hero,
better than Ned Kelly or ANZAC.
He died young and pretty
And entertained the masses.
I understand viciousness begets viciousness
And sometimes my callousness is a wack seamer*

    *right in the meat of the bat,
which missed the bouncer down the club
and killed former Australian and New South Wales
Sheffield Shield """"First Class"""" player, Robert Barclay.
All generations are war generations. There is only defeat
in this sallow, devolving universe.*

    *I was never a Koolie kid,
just a bullet-ridden messenger, reporting
to spoiled Daddy-pressured boys*

that they were dropped from cricket.
A cricketer is dead. He was not a racehorse,
not a poverty-stricken athlete
with no other skills.
    Not a woman, side-eying yes all men.
He was twenty-five and Anglo and died doing what he loved.
    There is nothing to like, mourn?
At twenty, I couldn't stomach mourning
any more privileged people.
    Cool my black heart.
There is nothing to like, mourn?
    A cricketer is dead.
But alas my soul returns
Bludgeoned!
Earth's Endless Glee.
RIP Robert Barclay
Luv, the Return of Teenage Me
Pre-Ungenred-Tragedy.

Gravey White Concerns (Suicide Order)?

Yes, you are right
my father was White
but I said I was never a Koolie kid
so I have to ask
are you trying
to claim his remains

long since fresh
from the casket
where his bones rest
in Rouse Hill?
are you trying to drive
a wedge between
my brown skin
and a corpse of a beloved
I never visit
Or is it our souls you want?
Segregate the masses of brown people
and friends who are coming for you,
who would have liberated you too
had you not backed yourself
into a spineless grave
with no dark soil
to cover what coloured
people do not care
if you reveal
or conceal: the shit
riches of your garden beds
are yours, but
There is no longer
a burden for you
to share.

Fresh Cold Berserk (Whiteness Interruptus)

I am pantless and shirtless and beflabbed
    between unwashed sheets
in the drudgery of the vague morning sheen.
Circadian rhythms have improved
inside the cocoon of current carnivorous jaunt
und nasium bent. I am warmed
    but I am late, for date imperativ.
Personal Training with Fate today.
Timetabled public transport is nigh.
    Sigh.
I wallow under blinding linen skin as the kookaburras
chase away magpies who chase away sparrows
who chase away worms who chase away
the local White baby boomers
concerned about their investments
that their privileged children do not even live in
because Oops! Didn't Know That Was a Thing.
I am a vagabond, a vagrant – indelibly, incredibly,
    adverbially stained
by the only true, virtuous skin I've ever known.
    Pillow Saccharino.
Euroclassic Pedestaline of my misshapen,
undernourished heart.
    socket squelch
Expelled, I am free of the shallowness,
free to outfox the day, unless I am dragged –

back to that Sherwood, Castle Peaks –
by a morbid, bestial power-shriek that is what I cannot shake,
ever-present, like threats –
not Christmas threats, socks made of coal or potato
the solitary gift some annual Sack Do affords –
mine man-cloak that I always seem to wear, 'unlawful' identity.
    This^.
Shower, exfoliation. This is my contemplation nation
I hippy-skippy to the nearest train station.
Glower, abomination. The Sydney train is late.
    Shun.
I live Out West – in beauteous exile
from inner-suburban defilement –
but I am
summat-quite-thing fond
o' this Tiggr mess of a system.
It glistens ridicurrous. Boing, boing, herp!
IT
'Saemson — Pummel O'Dreadlockson? Is that you?'
Jayzus, mate!
I just.
Cannot.
Shun.
    These^.
Old Mate eats a puffy, fluffy creamed-corn pie
atop a cream cake atop a muffin top:
'I could *really* use a big spork right about now,
Pummel, old pal.'
    Old Mate's done it now.
I am beskinned in names of his and Fate's previous
choosing (destiny, not my PT. Sigh.)
We used to choose life together

before that fateful summer's storm
come and torn our bits into even shardier nano-style,
pictorial pieces.
Pillow invited Old Mate and The Normies to the carnival
but I only received a late, token, second-hand invitation.
Glint, asunder.
Assumed Jealousy and Brokenness
rather than standard annoyance
@ weird, unnecessary rudeness.
Shit. Missed calls. The Remains of Personal Training Day.
3 Missed Calls: Fate (PT – not destiny. Sigh)
'You probably haven't heard.
About The One We Called Pillow? You missed
our graduation reunion dewaxing anti-hazing excursion –
your ears must be so cloggo right now, champ?
But I digress, deliberately –
to erase Pillow, momentarily, while speaking of her –
so as to maintain blissful selfhood!
future-proofing my past into a deliberate lower-case
erasing it slowly, being present.
Sorry, if I am currently erasing your present...'
Old Mate's talk, familiar yet distant,
to thine, unmedicated me
without asking, corralled me
into an enclosure
that this Zuckerman's famous durable pig
would endure willingly, and only then was This Old Pig
forced to endure the unendurable, vague elliptical
chaotic-prosaic-mosaic of this UnCharlotte's Exit-Web.
Pillow, ya gawn. Can deal. Yawn.
traffic noise, morning bougie footpath clops
    Pillowww!
'She is locked in dread – grieved and shocked and
schlocked with a medical condition.'

Pillowwww. Vulnerablllllloooow. Like meee — finally.
And will understand. The. Shape. Of. Water. Or. You.
Or acute, non-whimsical non-merperson pain.
'The Probbo Past Remains Groundhoggy
for my Decisionny Baddiness too, not to worry,' said Old Mate.
'Ego repetition yields power to previous reputation.'
Again? Oh yeah, haunting ay bro...
Fixed alternate-pronoun beleaguers
my non-actual man-cloak, the boyhood,
so problematic and tight and rigid,
like the over-starched briefs
of a 1950s-style cis-het American office worker who
blames his cis-het-female life partner
for life's every fresh ellipses-analepsis outsourcery.
    Misericordia. Mise-en-scene. Man and his dirty bed.
The Case of the Lost Future Comfort.
    Pilllloooooowwwww. Noooo.
Grew. Apart. Grew. Up. Too. Soon. Despite.
Extended. CHILDHOOD.
'Oh, O'Dreadlock?'
Old Mate Relapse. Solitary. Apartment. Midnight. Oil. Lyrics.
Foundational insomnia caused by...
Pillooow...head-whispery...plaintive...whimsical...itis.
    Sigh. I used to conch in this stream.
Oi, Dreddy, bringing tree-change nostalgia
World War Two? Go Beach haunt holiday?
Rewound tape hallucination from pornographic trauma:
Old Mate's face, pure cream sans pastry-ness
and human parts, cobbed by its own corn.
Regals me. *IT!* I forget my dignity forever – no resume, no
relationships, no ability to reflect and learn.
And plough backwards.
Back towards Castle Peaks again.
Towards the fresh, cold void of climactic Berserkitude.

Except, I baulk @ the Sisyphus Hill.
I hear a bus blistering, engine-like, industrially,
recalling ham sandwiches in modest, pre-Howard-Era
Castle Peaks underbelly tuckshops.
Split. Mango. Dingo.
Infinite adjectiv.
'Sorry Mister Poltergiest, you're one pus-ridden
blisterhand
I will neither pick nor shake.
'M'Ayo!'
The summer climate steadied to comfortable, light breeze
hair-dryer and I could not help gazing backwards,
a blissful alternative, moment-sojourn.
'Bit harsh?' cried Old Mate. 'But – Pillow: I figured you'd
want to know – she almost croaked. Of lung cancer –
'Oi, Dreddy, bringing tree-change nostalgia
World WarTwo? Beach haunt holiday?' –
that spread, from toe cancer. Remember all Dem Durries?
Dose Bevvies? Dat Pepsi Max Diet?
Da Fat-Free muffins baked on her Sickies?
Our volatile figures in the light that are now only shadows
to box only when constantly mentioned. Mate?'
'Manchild – please,' I said with unclenched, skyward palms
hiding the caramel-latte melanin product knuckle-glaze.
'You don't even have to mention Mauritius,
but kindly Shove off, Old Mate.'
'*Suf-fer!*' said a gleeful student rando in Adidas singlet,
Kappa pants, bent-legged in one Nike shoe
and one New Balance shoe, all hanging out the bus window
by a rope of several school ties.
At least I'm not the only one who got tagged
back in the day.
I board – sit down, humble but brittle, on the M54 bus,
which humdrums to the shopping centre

that you'll know if you're in the private-know.
It stands upright and forthright
amidst mild, bristle-bustle sprawl that bears my birth-name.
I contemplate Old Mate contemplating
public human rights battles in private.
Because he gets it now. Understood
IT
Mr Unplough, that name again, somehow, though I never
inexorably uttered...
IT
Before
'God, so wish I was a Sino-Indian beetle.
Anyone but
This^!'
I volunteer, as I once did with my time,
with children who were not my own,
but were my own self-childhood erasure –
except this was not sneaky-cheese metaphor,
it was aloud, to the wrinkly bronze baby boomer
bus driver's knowing, inviting, lolling grin
in the mirror of the empty metal carriage.
His old Golden Retriever doggo hiss-whined like bad brakes.
Only then did I notice the lovely mutt's frosty froth
next to its head on the rubber-lino-whatever floor.
'Next stop is Real Hart Lane!
It'll be busy, chap. The festival is on.
In Australia, best be avoiding the cool quick-stickery
you might not understand.
Be not offended in my upending of ya – yeah, boi?'
The bus driver toothed a giant custard apple,
gripped with vigour,
spat out the juicy, coloured skin
into a scrunched, brown paper bag
as I somehow read my latest text by unverified osmosis

while staring at him, sweating everywhere
but especially in my unexposed pits
and on the hair on my temples:
'I can no longer train you, Sameson. Must cancel indefinitely.
My cat's grandy is unwell and needs my full, undivided
professional attention...forever!
Rgds, F.'
Thank you
And Fffff *I...*
'*Saemson. Soz! :)'
...T
Aftershock
Entire childhood monoculture was
Alternate, deflection? Pontificating procrastinator...matez?
Uncle Leo Un-Hello-ers?! Agony
Grandma Pure, bigoted microaggression or
Impure, Grandpa indignant macroaggression?!

Let thou (he)art be in-between
and left lean, cringing
culturally;

Togethie

Recognis-epiph
Siesta-steeled commute
Heart-graffiti

Luv, Teenage Frayston Bond Withergoon-Leatherskin

Thirsty

No-one dies of hunger
While I am distracted
Fake thirst,
racialised, playing
@ individuality
a man benefitting
from hetero backbone,
close to queer intimacy
with animal instincts
trapped
in a war-shot
viewfinder.
I am an animal
Can't you tell?
Cast as fake animal
'bout to burst.
Animus, anima
Subtract the tame
It's just a game
and we're whistle-blown refs
ignoring searing shame and blame
Not speaking loud or kindly enough.
Imposter Syndrome!
Imported, downloaded
By dirty cheats
And their omnipresent gift
Oversharing a mix
o' derision and scorn
Spilling over their own rage
A hate-porn selfie

greed, chest-beating
barbarians o' bloodlust fun.
Calling out bias while
projecting a bias
towards...
YOU
Won't protect what you've done.
I played @ being a thirsty wolf
as a joke
in all the wrong ways –
well, some, wrong for me –
To cover unhealing
of my goad-scar past
To cover what I hated,
my shambolic story
Reality Farce!
I don't want to (self-)judge
Don't want to embitter
But also
I'm 'fessing my beast life
RIP,
too much unplanned, serrated
roaring-twenties me.
Nice, even boring,
underrated,
I feared being feared.

Fragments of Doom

culling doom
I shun city grooves
bound up the rugged m1,
left lane to not get grunted
In the wash
harsh defrag of last night's munted, dirt-faced soldiers
capital mines and renovated homes,
charged together, tacky tack-ons,
turtles or squashed crabs on White plates
castigating higher powers of the shapeless dunes
and sullied plastic oceans. I am a metal-mouthed fish, fuck –
backseat toddlers, limbs sprawling,
dogs on trays leashed and unleashed
a hundred and ten Ks and I am hooked,
blown into a town that relies on blow-ins but doesn't want to,
ornate suburban dust in the art gallery
of blocked white on sunshine yellow paintings
but at least I'm in the queue.

Rogans Hill Mutt (Hello My Koolie)

My landlord is away
Adult boy-girl twins will play
Dommie and Liv kids
Now take out the lids
On pink-skied Thursday eves,
Durries and McFlurries.
And took in a mutt
from Rogans Hill.
Named it Beardy
And nicknamed it Seedy.
And joked he looks like me.
They partied in law,
band next door
Until their parent-bosses got 'em
for the dogs' howl.
A sting, gutful grime
A garage barrage, banned too
The Hedgebetters! But
gambled the lot
Gutless gusto, unglued.
So I will scrub myself
And bust my tanking guts
to hound only truth,
not one-ups
not pats on backs
not vanity cards
o' beauty and nobility
and Western Civilization

or (Anti-)virtuoso-signalling,
not Westie brothers'
candescent warmth,
for people's truth
denied too long,
disguised in alcohol ads
Tree Change Drama Glory!
Bringing People Together
to control the other's story
And don't forget the glass-clink pseudo-purity
of pre-wasted
Cheers. And as I yell
Compartmentalise, Kids!
I know Boundaries,
(un)hit
Is all the young ones can do
Forced to fight,
slick instincts
fending off
(C)rumbling Global World
Energy at-large! Edges, edges
Beaches drenched
Sinking islands
@-us
Boundaries
To undo
Generations.

Mongrel

Unlock this muted Castle Peaks mongrel
Flowerdaze, duckpond *placebos* in Dural
and Campsie gazebos. Feeding halos of greed,
sleek gravestones, traversing
"blights with plague the marriage hearse"
and "best minds of my generation"
to find only knock-knock jokes, homez? Doors
Plus, vengeful Whiteboys keying cars and vaping,
expansion mansions, maintenance men
claiming durry culture and curry munching,
Leicester Square, Scarborough Fair laid bare.
Confronting, ya know? Exactly that. Screaming from behind
brick veneer walls craving openness, what if
we were opened @ conception, admitting
man-made charades, atomising holographic fragments,
knocking blandness — just rock steady, flat moors,
flat moods, unapocalyptic. Unapologetic. Sky-write,
true-blue vanilla chem-trailers. Top-spun highwire
ain't everyls cuppa,
tech-tonic earth shakes cliff face
bold underlings donning shades.
Kind tradie malaise, crowded Domain, your mate my plate,
buying propaganda, switch off.

->->-> KIN AND KIND

Folks

My mother is a kind of anti-hero, my father, wunder-martyr-kind
Now I breakfast on basa curry
sans sea view, an Aldi delicacy, Parramatta suburbs
And live among hidden White fish.
I married my parents on our breakfast bar,
3 years old and 3ft tall,
head scraping no ceiling spiders,
no unclean webs, workaholic world
Looking back, I eat, eat, destroying
all effigies and memories, favourites
people who all let go too soon. I laugh,
spoon nerves and too-raw curry sauce
Dancing @ my parents' wedding reception, musty
Rhodes cottage, my grandmother's inheritance,
arms flailing, baby droid dancing, blue bowtie,
tight white shirt, under a cut-price marquee
Taught to lead girls out
o' dancefloor shyness, share what's yours Simba,
marshmallows melting fire, be gentle and clear. Crashes o'
my uncle's cymbals, burning Koolie memories. Live
Older cousins and family-friends vote
blood rushes, bullrush and hidings,
truth or dare over our tricycles and soccer balls.
Lush '80s nostalgia, panacea panacea
I remain stubborn, still dancing, stiff legs.
Sharp, backyard grass
spikes my ankles
I struggle to find soft drinks
Office workers, not uncles or aunts drunk
douse their sweaty cheeks under Pa

and Nan's garden hose, pushing Mauritian cousins
down rough, grass cement driveway
Splintery skateboard wheels shunt forward
slow over old cracks. Mama and Papa's
first official dance: Matilda in utero still
I was an experimental mix, limited edition
Sick: cake and lollies and soft drink
And pretending I achieved @everything, even dancing,
proving brown-kid worthiness. Austerity,
Novelty, Endless Work. I shuffled
In the front seat, promoted – Mum craved space
in the backseat to rest, not sleep
after the rigmarole, after the wedding-show,
dress shed, still in blazer, contact lenses
Your choice, voters - non-White: hot or not?
I guess her pressures. Or something else,
something not other. I can burn
belly fat, stop my hoarding, but
I still live in a fatuous promise:
Australian avarice.

Hospital Gods

Musty carpet 2004, mattresses slung on my shoulders.
I could have moved furniture all night,
Dull Impending Brain Damage.
Matilda and I camped on our parents' Queen bed often.
Now pastel blue and green plastic water cups and thin pyjamas,
four brown bodies heated to boiling point,
January air-conditioning hum
sailing our cooked skin flakes. Main bedroom, ensuite.

Window pane sheathed by White lacy curtains,
second storey: palm trees, pool and green plastic net
top the unfinished pagola and fairy light globes smashed,
Dad's backyard cricket drives. I flicked the switch,
ritual of the hallway night-light complete,
> *upturned conical lampshade*

aims @ stars, hitting cobwebbed ceilings.
Campsie to Castle Peaks — why is Nana watching this? I can't
reckon Mum's face as she folds the summer sheet down,
firm confident hands still, tributary veins flowing knuckle to wrist,
repelling engagement and wedding rings, firm together,
black Target tracksuit carrying sturdy legs
disappearing beige linen, right side, radio clock side, alarm side
> *where Dad would*

The hospital gods will call us, results.
Nana flushed, rushing sink-water
like Victoria Falls in National Geographic,
> *or Niagara in Superman II.*

I lay on the floor.

Unlocks Door

Unlit. Silent nothing,
no whistling or tickling breeze.
I mouth-snort,
release dark neck-apple tension. How-oooool!
Nana's scattered alarm, galaxy
gust above our beds. I hinge awake, Nosferatu-face, coffinless.
My chest and torso tighten again,
fend off sheet,

her words (un)clear
beyond my reckoning. Nana brushes thin
red-black hair off thinner scowl, hides tear stains.
Mum and Matilda groan in their sleep,
unmoved, absorbing expelled wounds. I drop
backwards, attempting sleep, awkward measure, levered
by strap and crane, adjusting quarry dreams.
Silent nothing. Dreading
hospital call, speaking, everything from above.
Face sticking linen again, I blow cool
air onto face sweatlets from the corners of my mouth, and flap
sheets over my cheeks and chest,
fan dream flames off sleeping lioness kisses.

Sad Song City

Back to 20yo, fambam holiday
after Dad went kaboom.
In deep shit, Empire ruins
(de)colonial waters
Fish are boring!
Coral reefs
endangering
ego spikes,
attention span
Fuck I am so bored
No, not bored
This island
This water
I am not H'Exotic

like *them*.
I need American shit,
British bands are as good
if not better.
In Boredom
I shoot myself, White bullets.
I am on the hotel bed
Stomach on mattress
legs in the air, heels up first
Renewal, rejecting real renewal
Forgetting who I am
And remembering at the same time
The brutal nothingdust
of bullshit eternal now
Today isn't yesterday
Or tomorrow
It's fucked – now
I've thought about it
Overthinking boy
who can be bothered
Lighten up, fuck
What am I gonna do with Enlightenment
Pretend to sail a yacht
Pretend to not be sullied by what I used to be?
Grief Mk II, I was an old White man
Or a young White woman
In Mauritius
Bored and sullen
And grrrrrrrrr
Aaaaaaahhh
Just another 20yo male here
Zzzzzzzzzzz

Craving Creole Curry House

I'm not your safari, just balmy
an architrave, crook-hook – styling stars
into a routine, takeaway
sharma, dream-sip Pondicherry
Seychelles, Afrique
flaming fillets charcoal, broth
grounds salty
to disappear
to belong,
Freak.
Map myself,
lose myself
Repeat
…

Florent Returns

Fragments of whistling sand
upon breezy, matted mounds
sewn by rising oceans
I am bustled, hustle dreams.
Dozing, counting clouds,
coconut flakes. Barren mountains drifting,
head on Nana's hunched shoulder,

KFC-ad lullabies. Red letter daze
->
Hurried entrance, Uno/Ludo wizards @ Grand Baie,
Papa's sister's bungalow breeze,
bent palm trees. Pebblecrete: *honk!*
Road rage @ Castle Peaks. Driveway, ambulance.
Catatonic, hospital waiting room,
cold veiny hands, tubes, grandparents watch the green flat line
Awake! I am bleak sunshine.
No boat trip, #Rodrigues
What is #Mauritius without parents, anyway?
Aman! iPod shuffle, sugar
and glass museums.
Taxi driver waits without air-con
Tears in the bistro under the ceiling fan
Jug of Coca-Cola, ice. Spillage
on the floral white, frills and napkins
'Eat, eat, babies!'
Giant macarons and achard. L'herbe?
No salad. Nana avec sister Matilda in the sega dress,
Blue and white floral, twin cultures.
Younger sibling, wiser for some reason
Escape! Scorsese montage. Mental,
driven, eat more: coconut juice, dholl puri
Success! Seize ans! Time to fly. 'Florent!'
Nana instructs: 'Girls everywhere, bebe!'
->
'Um...what's the deal with the Y2K bug?'
I say to the concierge,
peach hotel dress, Coke bottle glasses
Perfect Creole and French, broken English.
This ruddy chipmunk teleported
Archipelagic Magic, skin of our arms bubbling
in the hammock, head curls

unruly, madness in dreadlocked time.
Drop a selfie with Anju, inert. Flash!
A moment stolen, fresh for brain-scoop-agram.
Phone to muddy Rosehill turf,
Mum's distant swimming hole, gene pool.
Volleyball captain, scholar
took us to South Cronulla and The Entrance
and reminds us that she can't swim,
and reminds me she can't fly, not that way.
Anju grabs my phone –
Sticky Anglos scurry hearts
on our round-cheek smiles
in boxes, behind screens –
and puts it down her dress.
I excuse myself, cheap case
of Phoenix beers, esky ice, ignore thigh vibration.
Arrive late to the table, sedate, eyeballs still
But in one shaking piece, cut-off jeans
->
Foo Fighters T-shirt and Colorados
bought for work experience at CL
'Prawn *rougaille, faratha,* only. *Merci.*'
In the specious sun, procrastinating,
more memes and poses
and Facebook posts
More trips to crystalline waters and feasts
And sterile shonky Westerners clogging
and hollering on the bistro dancefloor,
howling @ the mirror-ball. Faeces! Sparkling fess-pee, sa.
Damages on TV, I hate that stinkin' ass show. Sorry
I cleanse in the bistro basin, water beads on hot sweat.
Nana is chirpy and assured,
'Phone buzz, no fuss!' and laughs.
I cave, more biryani and chicken curry, 'Co-ka-coh-la?!'

I squirm in my seat, Creole and French rain,
I pocket-mash. Phone sa, that aching device,
HURLS random kazoo melody,
@ the whole Grand Baie bistro, @ sega for the tourists,
I hit hashtag intruder, hit American cat
paws, jump-cutting, pause
and blue-grey stare,
Da-der-der-da-da-der-der-dada-dada-der
I register floppy plush oversized earphones,
exactly like Dad's costume hat 4 Tonton's parties.
Room stops, stares
I tap my own phone screen.
'*FLORENT*!'
all Nana says, mock outrage
'*Ayo, bubba*!' echoes, unsaid
incredulous eyebrows jiggling
up forehead creases, grinning piano mix
rotten and false teeth. So lovely
Stampede, music continues, voluntourists
sent to party, quell White Working Class rebels.
Sit my ass down.
I am an internet cat, stuck,
in, jump-cuts, Dodo T-Shirt, beer, Creole bistro.

Being Mauritian (Love You Sick)

I choose happiness, joie de vivre forever
though you cannot, not always
Though you didn't want to go with me
or Matilda
to Europe or Africa or even the RSL with the family
when we had the chance.
Full of YTs, I realised, who ignore or force you
to accept some bastardised version
I will always come back
It is easier now you are sick, I admit
I never compared your rage to an animal or machine
A tiger
Or an elephant
Or a helicopter
In cartoon poetic rhetoric. Though
No-one got close to you in argument
And the cyclones that move around us
Moved around you in your youth
Could not hurt me under your roof
Bending back but not breaking coconut palms
I had nothing to confess to any priest, any institution
Then or now
But I am not a blank slate or a White canvas
to slap chiaroscuro acrylics upon.
I will Answer Every Question
Even it creates more questions, for me at least
Sometimes they will hate my innocence
Even more than my experiences

that they have never had
My reluctance to act like them
Project in any way
Deficiency, slowness
Smartphones slowed down
by conspiratorial execs

->->-> HUNTED WHILE ADULTING

Whiteness

You wreck me
Every time
I find
Love
I find
Your gleaming
lit
demon
teeth
Haunting
Hunting
Every selfie
A car chase
Each new
Haircut
Headshot
Unmoored By
Heartfelt Memes
About Our World
A Police State
Articulate
Politicians
droogs and noobs
faking obsoletion
gaunt outrage
online
Derision
For the whole
Fucking conversation
Outsourcing ourselves

Into boxes
Swiping away
guilt
@ porous
economic
pleasures
And I forget
the tennis
poetry
art
and cinema
friendship and music
parties
and
forget
Love
And when I
Finally
Chuck
The covers off
Blink back tears
Bin
Tissues
Chuck back
my phone
to the bed
From inside
the bathroom door
clean
halitosis mouth
shower
and shampoo
oily split hair
and arrive

at the
minus
15 kilos
That should never –
Back
@ Love
I can only
Stare
horrorshow
at the bewildered
Woman
in front of me:
"Ready to go?"

Old Sandstone House

I
...

II
scrambling across the strangling lawn
I lean forward into my hoodie pockets
new Autumn is a middle child here
this pebbled earth skirts dearth, this sibling
brother sweats the bus queue
to him, I'm stuck, still sinking sandstone
twisting a copper tap to refresh
dry aching, drooping face droplets
fake tears, bleakness not mine
I love, expand this heart park
heavy in dank protrusions, a convict rebellion
sitting in cafes convinced, scullion!
I eat sunshine, lawn loud and soft
Can you hear me? I am mobile, unmuffled.
More than dry clean digits
A M'Aussie! Koolie on-deck
pushed up and outta dank
tudes, sinking rhythms
glowing gold arm-skin
a lit vacancy, my chest cave.
I match my window brother,
hot rubber aisle tween us home

III
Shoulders built

on sandstone """"grudges""""
I am humble shadows
Bristling lawn secrets
Indian myna scuffles
cockatoo wreckage,
falling of bark shards
to fake flat earth.
Hiding between pages
And timetable apps
Dwelling populus shot
Palm burns robotic
Fuck fear coffins
Sleek shunting
Rock rap skin
Classical chagrin
It's just a building.
Go inside, unlock
rusty tongues
Dust off grins, congress

IV
I wanted to announce I have shut the gate
but my hands are still plastered, sucking
up against the rough terrain of autumn sandstone
and my spine is up against it too. Shoulder blades
though are massaged, car-keyed encounters
looming grey buildings, centring
wallflower park, stand centre-stage
No scaffold or shackle for lighting or leaf

V
what records do you keep close
sunlit daze, masking shadows?

is it surface or sediment
can we ply it as one sea stone?

VI
look I can tell you're bored
bleak happiness unbounded
glorified passive rock cottage
just tell me what you want
listen, tucked into windows
wrought sunken iron
deserted meadowless grass
I would be a statue too if you asked
see I would bound the staircase
grand old Parra shack
put up shut up.
I am boring
sleek blandness unlit

VII
I am ruled unreal time
husk of echo dust
mineral collision
staring at smooth wooden floor
afraid of noise
clutching necklace quartz
planning for unlikely fires

VIII
I can slam heavy zoo door
to make it click
I can shut gates to what's past
I can scrub or polish history to a grim shine
I can eat and chunder beef leaf and lawn

And I can too ignore
my own chores
my own random abdomen
dusty next-day drunk
(and bend myself elephant trunk
and salivate under still tongue)
still mind military precision
I can belt myself
into a hard-heart form
Sip wine from goblet
Leave canned brine shelved
I could also push this house close
leave this hell of fallen stalks
And I will
burn museum
burn museum, I
Wick and wax quick
Will
descend
singed
fingertips
to talk

IX
I will sleep easy
unbound stone
wrapped beach
matted silt
proof to all weather
inside or outside
a definite
welcome

X
barter x trouble
seductive
suction cup palms
clutch the wall
rainbow lizard, Sugar Beach
atomised tourist
a global fragment
lapping up sun
(selfie incarnate)
seed on rock on boulder
remove tongue
carve a heartstone
atop headstone
dig a sandpit
not a grave

XI
...

XII
Shaking off the shackles
Boyhood mud
Slung dogshit
I had to unlearn everything.

XIII
Still I lurk,
this house of folly
Eating dead stone, chalky residue
EYRAGHHHH
Because I am a sick Koolie
hardly fully

springboarding into unfat stacks
daring wreckagez, @-me bewildered
eye meat, bugging the fronting liners
for schism mix, boi
Pretend late-night gangsta
Comfort crawl-ball huggery
A Maccas run, chips dipped in rougaille sauce

XIV
Who – shot – the Macquarie – dodo?
(Argh, argh – Maggie Simpson)
in the back of the head
only skull and foot remain
bullet – brain
not died in shit, too fat
to scavenge against sailors
and English animals
Shot – in the back of the head.
I would weaponise compassion
But I am numbed –
by genocide
of a tasty, fleshy bird.
Don't foodies Instagram those
Succumbing, wiping off grease
Displaying paused momentary glory?
I wish I cared more about birds
Not to shoot them – in the back of the head
Or """"weaponise offence"""" @ newspaper articles
Or Instagram their cooked, golden skin
Because they have eyes, ears
and mouths, limbs like me

Ginsberg's Ectoplasm (Barrage Haunts the Creole Searcher)

Ravaged BOO
This still rapture
I am stunned
to gravestone
Pillared by style
Cracked
by daring angels
Unblinking hipsters
thoughts
Arid boil,
lush pour
Kiss me
Dead history!
I live
Tracking
War-Bling
Descent
Map down.
Lift Juggernaut: universal law

Knock (Nobody Ever Says Mauritian)

Sometimes when my mates and I
knocked each other
We knocked each other too far,
accidentally,
or for our own entertainment
and break our doors off they hinges,
as cheesy as it sounds.
Stored hingeless, broken door
lives in the garage,
while the boxed-in image
we have of each other
left beside the door in my granny flat
not part of the furniture,
useless, unornamental.
Nobody ever says Mauritian
It's not as joyous, lyrical as Ja-May-Ka! or Mad-Agass-Scar!
It could be the Hills Effect.
Like Noplacia –
or a White discovery
that's already been overtaken
and gone through their cult
to canon bullshit, draining it
of all value. Then they move on
to the next thing.
But people still
live there,
as cheesy as it sounds.

Smoke (Waiting for Paloma)

lung-suck moist night air, clutching
the chipped paint of the apartment railing
Nicotine, pot and crystal fumes
Consuming Baulkham Hills balcony
Errol revels in the fleeting high of the fog
I choke the vanishing sun
five-thirty sky sullied by
mango and peach blemishes.
Where are you, Pillow?
Paloma's parents' apartment. Errol?
Men are like stars not diamonds, Paloma texted back
Your value is not found in scarcity
Trick is not to get too close
Emoji appears in the text box: wide grin and gushing tears
I text back:
Smarty
->
'My dick,' Errol said, pursing his lips
on a glass pipe and blowing smoke
across the white plastic outdoor table straight @-me
'Lazy as me dad's dying ute tonight!'
This guy could do anything tonight,
judging actions, not words
I wish I held that thought that back then
But I sucked down pale ales –
avoiding racist conversation
about Paloma's mixed heritage
not outing her as like me –

on the balcony and later in the media-and-electronic
dominance of the lounge room. I ate more sugar
and fat than @ Nana's place when Mum wasn't watching
Waiting for Paloma.
->
'Has he...ODed?' asked a rando.
Paloma scoffed as we lugged Errol,
under one pungent armpit each
Through the wire-screen door of the balcony
Dropped him onto the beige micro-fibre corner-lounge
'Nah,' said Paloma, rubbing her brown basketballer's shoulders
through the wide neck of her purple blouse
'This ain't *Pulp Fiction*. Just needs sleep.'
->
Paloma cuddled my black hoodie, dozing
Errol groaned like a dying bull, six-foot-five frame merged
with the beige cushions before passing out.
Nobody drank, smoked or conversed much more
The moment, the night, was soured.
->
By two am, even the most dreary-eyed night-stressers slept
on lounges or in sleeping bags on the floor.
Paloma dragged all her brand-new couches,
delivered free by her parents despite her protests
'All fucking new-school, brah,' said Paloma, hugging herself
and wriggling within the self-embrace and scratching
@ her Hollywood-straightened black hair.
'I don't feel funky enough.'
I was sprawled on the corner lounge. Paloma now
curled up on its large chaise. We both were on Errol duty, unofficial
We three covered the beige lounge that Paloma despised
->
Almost crossing over into Hangover
I squinted through heavy chunks of dry sleep residue
a vaseline blur on my dirty glasses.

Errol flopped his arm around Paloma's wide, taut waist
covered only by her Macquarie University hoodie.
'Mmngh,' Paloma murmured and hit Errol's arm,
but it didn't budge.
I awoke to see Errol's arm between Paloma's legs,
    prying them apart
I stared, eyes half-open, paralysed.
Errol's arrow-shaped hand
slid into Paloma's pubic region,
pushing in and out with rhythm
'Do-on't,' Paloma said, faux-laughing,
wriggling and swatting him away,
on her stomach on the chaise, eyes closed.
    Then jumped to her feet
'Man, what the fuck?' said Paloma
'Yeah, what the – man?' I said
'*Oh-wut*? Shit,' said Errol. 'I'm out, hey.'
'Get gone,' said Paloma.
    I heard Errol's boots echo
        on the concrete steps in the corridor.
Paloma strode into the kitchen,
arms folded tightly hands cupped and hidden.
I followed and leant against the bench
near the whistling kettle.
'Did you want to...? I can say...what I saw, and everything,'
'Maybe,' said Paloma, nodding and squeezing my arm
on her way towards the fridge.
The light from the fridge bathed the kitchen in an alien sheen.
Paloma lit up, illuminating her nose and mouth
for a moment, taking a drag
and exhaling smoke out the kitchen window.
The molten tip of the cigarette was the only light in the apartment.
'Coffee?' said Paloma. Bogarting her ciggie,
muffling her voice. 'With bourbon or without?'

Into Other People's Cars

High school daze, Paloma
Passenger of Fate
prisoner of windowsill
not drunken on rage, or still
corralled into other
people's cars
driven @ dawn
prison @ dusk
will to escape drivers
that old birdsong
youthful protest
detest unreason
Are they able to see:
daybreak
and nightfall
ground feathers
leaves deadened
descent o' blood orange skins
happy brown scrapes
a tinge, a tearlet flood
mathematical eyes
impossibilities
made sound by
the warrior imp
songs to quake branches
bring birds home
Fried flowers for tea?
traipsing up trails

bushes and doofs are memorials,
massacres
just dry lyrics to them
Fails. Entrails
of vicious trips
in other
people's cars

Radical Kindness

take nothing you would not nurture threefold
as it cartwheels its way back to you
an accordion somersaulting
unfashionable rainbow trampoline
meadows unpicked truanting round
festering anger
pity and trauma
Fresh Carnival
@ dusk
Africultures Festival
alone
the first time
not the last time
I am kitten but human
batting spools
string theory
to knot your video heart.

ACKNOWLEDGEMENTS

Thanks and love to my teachers, editors and publishers, writers, readers, family, workmates and friends, especially in the North-West and South-West of Sydney. I hope we keep on reading—written words and each other.

ABOUT THE AUTHOR

Jason Gray is a Mauritian-Australian writer who writes about youth, being Xennial/Millennial, being bi-cultural, a Person of Colour, of forms of media, toxic/White patriarchal and restorative/progressive masculinity, displacement, suburbia and home and staying kind in this late (anti-)capitalist hellscape. Twitter @jasongray85

ABOUT SUBBED IN

Subbed In is a not-for-profit DIY literary organisation and small press based in Sydney, Australia. Subbed In's program of publications and events aim to elevate the voices of trans people, people of colour, non-binary people, sex workers, women, people with a disability, LGBTQIA+ people, First Nations people, survivors, working class people, and anyone who finds themselves on the margins of the supremely white, cis, heteronormative, capitalist, colonial, ableist, patriarchal hellscape in which we live.

For more information visit: *www.subbed.in*

ALSO AVAILABLE FROM SUBBED IN

When I die slingshot my ashes onto the surface of the moon
by Jennifer Nguyen

The Hostage
by Šime Knežević

If you're sexy and you know it slap your hams
by Eloise Grills

blur by the
by Cham Zhi Yi

wheeze
by Marcus Whale

Parenthetical Bodies
by Allison Gallagher

The Naming
by Aisyah Shah Idil

Girls and Buoyant
by Emily Crocker

www.ingramcontent.com/pod-product-compliance
Lightning Source LLC
Chambersburg PA
CBHW032049290426
44110CB00012B/1018